Crafting a Family Legacy: Incorporating Whole Life Insurance into Your Financial Plan

By: J. R. Glenn

Copyright: 2024

Chapter 1: Introduction to Whole Life Insurance
   Understanding Whole Life Insurance
   The Concept of Financial Banking Systems
Chapter 2: Using Dividend Whole Life Insurance from Mutual Companies
   What are Mutual Companies?
   Benefits of Dividend Whole Life Insurance
   Building a Family Banking System
Chapter 3: Strategies for Maximizing Dividend Payouts
   Factors Affecting Dividend Payments
   Policy Structure and Its Impact on Dividends
   Timing and Amount of Premium Payments
Chapter 4: Comparing Mutual Companies
   Key Players in the Market
   Evaluating Dividend History
   Assessing Financial Strength and Ratings
Chapter 5: The Role of Whole Life Insurance in Estate Planning
   Integrating Whole Life Insurance into Your Estate Plan
   Wealth Transfer Strategies
   Utilizing Death Benefits for Estate Liquidity
Chapter 6: Leveraging Cash Value from Whole Life Policies
   Understanding Cash Value Accumulation
   Utilizing Cash Value for Emergency Funds
   Impact of Withdrawals on Policy Health
Chapter 7: Tax Benefits of Dividend Whole Life Insurance

- Tax-Deferred Growth of Cash Value
- Tax-Free Death Benefit
- Tax Implications of Policy Loans

Chapter 8: Integrating Whole Life Insurance into a Family Financial Legacy Plan
- Defining Your Family Legacy Goals
- Aligning Whole Life Policies with Legacy Objectives
- Communication and Education for Family Members

Chapter 9: Understanding the Loan Features of Dividend Whole Life Insurance
- How Policy Loans Work
- Advantages and Disadvantages of Borrowing
- Repayment Strategies

Chapter 10: Building a Self-Funding Retirement Plan
- Utilizing Whole Life Insurance for Retirement Income
- Creating a Sustainable Withdrawal Strategy
- Balancing Policy Growth and Retirement Needs

Chapter 11: Risk Management with Whole Life Insurance
- Stabilizing Family Finances During Uncertain Times
- Whole Life Insurance as a Safety Net
- Long-term Financial Resilience

Chapter 12: Case Studies of Successful Financial Banking Systems
- Real-Life Examples of Infinite Banking
- Lessons Learned from Successful Policyholders
- Key Takeaways for Implementing Your Own System

Chapter 13: Conclusion
- Recap of Key Concepts
- Next Steps for Readers
- Encouragement for Building a Legacy

Recommendations:

Chapter 1: Introduction to Whole Life Insurance

Understanding Whole Life Insurance

Whole life insurance is a foundational component of many financial strategies, particularly for those seeking to create a sustainable legacy for their families. This insurance product, offered by mutual companies, provides not only death benefits but also a cash value component that grows over time, often with the potential for dividends. Understanding how whole life insurance functions is crucial for both life insurance agents and customers who want to leverage this financial tool effectively. The combination of guaranteed growth and dividends makes whole life insurance an attractive vehicle for building wealth and securing financial stability.

One of the key features of whole life insurance is its ability to accumulate cash value, which can be accessed for various financial needs. This cash value grows at a guaranteed rate, and many policies also pay dividends, which can be reinvested to enhance growth. For life insurance agents, it's essential to educate clients on the importance of maximizing dividend payouts, as these can significantly increase the policy's value over time. Clients should be encouraged to explore the various options for utilizing dividends, whether to reduce premiums, purchase additional coverage, or enhance cash value growth.

When comparing mutual companies that offer dividend whole life policies, several factors must be considered. Not all mutual companies are created equal in terms of their dividend performance, financial stability, and customer service. Life insurance agents must provide clients with comprehensive comparisons of different carriers to help them make informed decisions. This includes analyzing historical dividend payments, the company's financial ratings, and the overall benefits offered by different policies. A thorough understanding of these aspects can empower customers to choose a policy that aligns with their financial goals.

Whole life insurance also plays a pivotal role in estate planning and wealth transfer. The death benefit from a whole life policy can provide liquidity to heirs, ensuring that family assets are preserved and debts are settled without the need for liquidating other investments. Furthermore, the cash value can be strategically utilized to cover estate taxes, thereby protecting the family legacy. Life insurance agents should emphasize these benefits when discussing whole life policies with clients, highlighting how they can serve as a cornerstone of a comprehensive estate plan.

Finally, leveraging the cash value of whole life insurance for emergency funds and retirement planning is a strategy that can enhance financial security. The policyholder has the option to take loans against the cash value, providing immediate access to funds when needed. Additionally, incorporating whole life insurance into a self-funding retirement plan allows individuals to create a stable income stream while mitigating risks associated with market fluctuations. The tax benefits associated with whole life insurance, including tax-deferred growth and tax-free death benefits, further solidify its position as a vital component in a robust family financial legacy plan. Understanding these multifaceted benefits is essential for life insurance agents and customers alike, enabling them to craft effective financial strategies that endure across generations.

The Concept of Financial Banking Systems

The concept of financial banking systems revolves around the idea of creating a personal financial infrastructure that serves not only as a safety net but also as a platform for wealth accumulation and transfer. At the core of this system is dividend whole life insurance from mutual companies, which provides both a death benefit and a cash value component that grows over time. This dual structure allows policyholders to utilize their insurance policies as a financial tool, facilitating liquidity, investment opportunities, and risk management. By understanding how to effectively integrate whole life insurance into a broader financial strategy, families can establish a robust legacy that supports their long-term goals.

Maximizing dividend payouts is crucial in enhancing the effectiveness of whole life insurance as a financial banking system. Mutual companies often declare dividends based on their performance and policyholder participation. Life insurance agents can guide clients on strategies to boost these payouts, such as selecting the right policy structure, maintaining consistent premium payments, and understanding the implications of policy loans and withdrawals. The ability to accumulate significant cash value over time not only provides a source of funding for emergencies but also enhances the overall financial security of families, allowing them to navigate economic uncertainties with greater confidence.

When comparing mutual companies, it is essential to evaluate which providers offer the most advantageous dividend whole life policies. Factors such as historical dividend performance, financial strength ratings, and customer service play a significant role in this assessment. Life insurance agents should conduct thorough research and present clients with options that align with their financial goals. A well-chosen mutual company can lead to improved cash value growth and more substantial dividends, ultimately enhancing the effectiveness of the family banking system established through whole life insurance.

Whole life insurance also plays a pivotal role in estate planning and wealth transfer. By integrating whole life policies into a family financial legacy plan, families can ensure that their wealth is preserved and passed down efficiently to future generations. The tax benefits associated with whole life insurance, such as tax-deferred growth and tax-free death benefits, further enhance its value as an estate planning tool. Families can leverage the cash value of these policies not only to cover estate taxes but also to create a seamless transition of wealth that supports their heirs' financial needs.

In addition to serving as a cornerstone for wealth accumulation, whole life insurance provides essential risk management features that stabilize family finances. The predictable nature of whole life insurance premiums and the guaranteed death benefit offer families peace of mind in uncertain times. Furthermore, the ability to access cash value through policy loans provides an emergency fund that can be tapped without the need for traditional bank loans, fostering a self-funding retirement plan. By understanding and utilizing the loan features and benefits of dividend whole life insurance, families can create a resilient financial banking system that supports their needs today and secures their legacy for tomorrow.

Chapter 2: Using Dividend Whole Life Insurance from Mutual Companies

What are Mutual Companies?

Mutual companies are unique entities in the insurance landscape, primarily distinguished by their ownership structure. Unlike publicly traded companies, mutual companies are owned by their policyholders. This means that when individuals purchase whole life insurance policies from these organizations, they become members and co-owners, which can significantly influence how profits are distributed. The primary advantage of this structure is that mutual companies typically return a portion of their profits to policyholders in the form of dividends, enhancing the value of their whole life insurance products. This model aligns the interests of the company with those of its policyholders, creating a collaborative financial environment.

One of the most compelling features of whole life insurance from mutual companies is the potential for dividend payouts. These dividends can be used in various ways, such as purchasing additional coverage, reducing premiums, or increasing the policy's cash value. For life insurance agents and customers engaged in infinite banking, understanding how to maximize these dividends is crucial. Strategies may include selecting policies with favorable dividend histories, closely monitoring the company's performance, and strategically timing any policy adjustments. By leveraging these dividends effectively, policyholders can enhance their financial banking systems and ensure robust support for their families.

When evaluating mutual companies, it is essential to compare their dividend whole life policies to determine which offers the best value. Not all mutual companies have the same financial strength or dividend performance, and agents must guide clients toward policies that align with their financial goals. Key factors to consider include the company's historical dividend payout ratios, its financial stability, and the overall performance of its investment portfolio. Thorough research and analysis can help clients make informed decisions that will benefit their long-term financial planning and legacy objectives.

Whole life insurance plays a vital role in estate planning and wealth transfer strategies. As a financial tool, it not only provides a death benefit but also accumulates cash value over time, which can be leveraged during the policyholder's lifetime. This cash value can be tapped into for emergency funds or as a source of retirement income, offering flexibility that traditional savings methods may lack. Furthermore, the tax benefits associated with whole life policies make them an attractive option for long-term savings, enabling families to build wealth while minimizing their tax liabilities.

The loan features of dividend whole life insurance are particularly advantageous for individuals looking to build a self-funding retirement plan. By borrowing against the policy's cash value, policyholders can access funds without triggering a taxable event. This feature creates a unique opportunity for financial planning, allowing families to maintain liquidity and access capital as needed, all while preserving their wealth within the policy. Through case studies of successful financial banking systems using whole life insurance, it becomes evident that these strategies not only stabilize family finances but also create a lasting legacy that can be passed down through generations.

Benefits of Dividend Whole Life Insurance

Dividend whole life insurance offers a unique blend of benefits that can significantly enhance a family's financial strategy. One of the primary advantages is the guaranteed death benefit combined with the potential for dividends, which can provide a stable and predictable income stream. This dual benefit is particularly appealing for families looking to ensure financial security for their heirs while also having the opportunity to grow their cash value over time. The dividends, typically paid by mutual insurance companies, can be reinvested, used to pay premiums, or taken as cash, making this insurance product versatile for various financial needs.

Utilizing dividend whole life insurance within a financial banking system can allow families to create a self-sustaining financial ecosystem. By leveraging the cash value of their policies, families can access funds for emergencies, investments, or major expenses without relying on external financing options. This strategy not only preserves capital but also reinforces the policy's value, as the loan taken against the cash value does not require repayment within a specific timeframe, allowing for flexible financial management. This self-funding capability empowers families to take charge of their financial futures.

Maximizing dividend payouts is another critical aspect of dividend whole life insurance. Policyholders can enhance their dividends through careful selection of mutual companies known for their strong financial performance and consistent payout history. By comparing various mutual companies, agents can guide clients toward policies that not only align with their financial goals but also offer the best potential returns. This choice is crucial as it directly impacts the overall growth of the cash value and the death benefit, making thorough research and analysis imperative.

Incorporating dividend whole life insurance into estate planning and wealth transfer strategies can provide significant tax advantages. The death benefit is generally paid out free of income tax, enabling families to pass on wealth without the burden of tax liabilities. Additionally, the cash value grows tax-deferred, allowing policyholders to accumulate savings while minimizing tax exposure. This feature makes dividend whole life insurance an attractive option for those looking to build a lasting family legacy while strategically managing tax implications.

Finally, dividend whole life insurance serves as an essential tool for risk management in stabilizing family finances. By providing a guaranteed death benefit and a growing cash value, it acts as a safety net during unforeseen circumstances. Families can rest assured knowing that their loved ones will have financial support in times of need. This peace of mind is invaluable, enabling families to focus on long-term financial planning and wealth accumulation, thereby reinforcing the role of whole life insurance as a cornerstone of a comprehensive financial legacy plan.

Building a Family Banking System

Establishing a family banking system using dividend whole life insurance from mutual companies provides a robust framework for financial stability and growth. At its core, this system allows families to leverage the cash value accumulated in their whole life policies to support various financial needs without relying solely on traditional banking institutions. By treating the whole life insurance policy as a financial asset, families can create a self-sustaining banking system that funds education, real estate purchases, or other significant investments. This approach not only enhances financial literacy within the family but also instills a sense of responsibility and planning among its members.

To maximize the benefits of a family banking system, understanding how to optimize dividend payouts in whole life insurance is crucial.

Each mutual company offers different dividend rates based on their financial performance, so selecting the right provider is essential for maximizing returns. Families should regularly review their policies and compare the performance of various mutual companies to ensure they are receiving competitive dividends. By reinvesting dividends into the policy, families can accelerate cash value growth, enhancing the overall effectiveness of their family bank. This proactive approach allows families to adapt their financial strategies as market conditions change.

The role of whole life insurance in estate planning and wealth transfer cannot be overstated. By incorporating whole life policies into an estate plan, families can ensure that wealth is preserved and passed on efficiently. Whole life insurance provides liquidity to cover estate taxes and other obligations, allowing heirs to inherit assets without the burden of immediate financial pressures. This aspect of a family banking system reinforces its value as a tool for long-term financial planning, ensuring that future generations can benefit from the wealth created by their predecessors.

Leveraging the cash value from whole life policies serves as a strategic method for building emergency funds. Unlike traditional savings accounts, the cash value of a whole life policy grows at a guaranteed rate and can be accessed through policy loans for emergencies or unforeseen expenses. This feature not only provides financial security but also allows families to avoid the pitfalls of high-interest debt. By utilizing their family banking system, families can maintain their financial independence and stability, ensuring that they are prepared for any financial challenges that may arise.

In conclusion, integrating whole life insurance into a family financial legacy plan creates a powerful framework for building a family banking system. By understanding the loan features, tax benefits, and risk management aspects of dividend whole life insurance, families can establish a resilient financial foundation. This system not only supports immediate financial needs but also sets the stage for long-term wealth accumulation and preservation. As families engage in this process, they create a legacy that embodies their values and provides future generations with the tools to thrive financially.

Chapter 3: Strategies for Maximizing Dividend Payouts

Factors Affecting Dividend Payments

Factors affecting dividend payments in whole life insurance are crucial for both life insurance agents and infinite banking customers to understand, as these elements directly influence the financial viability of using these products as part of a broader financial strategy. First and foremost, the financial performance of the mutual insurance company plays a significant role in determining the dividend payouts. Companies that operate on a mutual basis are owned by policyholders, which means that any surplus earnings can be distributed in the form of dividends. Therefore, assessing the company's investment returns, expenses, and overall financial health is essential when evaluating potential dividend yields.

Another important factor is the policyholder's participation in the mutual company's surplus. Each policyholder's dividend is often based on their policy's size and the duration for which it has been held. This means that agents must communicate the importance of consistent premium payments and long-term commitment to policyholders, as these elements can directly enhance the overall dividend experience. By fostering this understanding, agents can help clients recognize the value of patience and dedication within their whole life insurance strategies.

Investment strategy also plays a crucial role in dividend payments. Mutual companies typically invest in a diversified portfolio of assets, including bonds, stocks, and real estate. The success of these investments can significantly impact the dividends paid out to policyholders. When agents analyze and compare policies among various mutual companies, they should focus on the investment strategies employed and historical performance, as these factors will influence future dividend distributions. A company with a robust investment approach may provide more favorable dividend outcomes over time.

Market conditions can further influence dividend payments. Economic factors, such as interest rates and inflation, can affect the profitability of the mutual company's investments. For instance, low-interest rates may lead to lower returns on fixed-income investments, which can subsequently reduce dividend payouts.

Agents should stay informed about market trends and educate clients on how external conditions can impact their whole life insurance policies.

Lastly, regulatory changes can also affect dividend payments. Insurance companies are subject to state regulations that may dictate how dividends are calculated and distributed. Life insurance agents should be aware of any legislative changes that could impact their clients' policies. By keeping abreast of these factors, agents can provide more effective guidance to clients, ensuring that they maximize their dividend potential while incorporating whole life insurance into their broader financial legacy plans.

Policy Structure and Its Impact on Dividends

Policy structure in dividend whole life insurance significantly influences the dividends policyholders receive, ultimately impacting their financial strategies. Mutual companies, which are owned by policyholders, often provide a more favorable dividend structure compared to stock companies. The policy features, such as premium payment terms, death benefit amounts, and cash value accumulation rates, play a crucial role in determining the overall dividend payouts. Understanding these structures allows agents and customers to effectively select policies that align with their financial goals and legacy planning.

One essential aspect of policy structure is the way dividends are calculated and distributed. Mutual companies typically base their dividend payouts on the performance of their investments, mortality costs, and administrative expenses. Consequently, a well-structured policy that prioritizes a strong cash value can lead to higher dividends over time. Agents must educate their clients on how these factors interact within their chosen policies to maximize dividend potential, emphasizing the importance of selecting the right company with a proven track record of consistent payouts.

In addition to the inherent features of the policy, strategic planning plays a vital role in maximizing dividend payouts. Policyholders can utilize strategies such as paid-up additions, which allow them to increase their death benefit and cash value. This not only enhances the policy's growth potential but can also lead to higher dividends in subsequent years. Agents should work closely with clients to develop personalized strategies that consider their long-term financial objectives, ensuring that the policy structure supports their goals for wealth transfer and emergency funding.

Comparing mutual companies is crucial when assessing which offers the best dividend whole life policies. Each company has its own approach to dividend distribution, influenced by its investment strategy and financial health. By analyzing factors such as historical dividend performance, financial strength ratings, and customer service, agents can guide clients toward companies that align with their preferences and financial needs. This comparison helps clients make informed decisions that will bolster their financial banking systems and support their family's legacy.

Finally, the policy structure's impact extends beyond immediate financial benefits; it plays a significant role in estate planning and wealth transfer. A well-structured whole life insurance policy can provide not only a death benefit but also a source of liquidity for heirs, helping to manage estate taxes and ensuring a smooth transition of wealth. By integrating whole life insurance into a family financial legacy plan, policyholders can leverage its features to create a lasting financial foundation for future generations, illustrating the profound impact of policy structure on dividends and overall financial stability.

Timing and Amount of Premium Payments

Timing and amount of premium payments are crucial factors in maximizing the benefits of dividend whole life insurance. For life insurance agents and infinite banking customers, understanding how these elements interact can significantly enhance the effectiveness of a financial banking system. Premium payments should be aligned with individual financial goals, cash flow, and the specific structure of the whole life policy. By carefully planning the timing of these payments, policyholders can ensure that they are optimizing the cash value growth and dividend payouts, which are essential for building a sustainable family legacy.

The amount of premium payments directly impacts the policy's cash value accumulation and the dividends generated. Higher premium payments often lead to a faster buildup of cash value, which can then be leveraged for loans or other financial needs. For agents, educating clients on the benefits of making larger, consistent premium payments can foster a more robust financial strategy. Conversely, clients with tighter budgets may need guidance on how to manage their premiums effectively while still reaping the benefits of whole life insurance. This might involve exploring flexible payment options offered by mutual companies or adjusting the payment frequency to suit their financial situation.

Timing is equally important in relation to policy dividends. Many mutual companies pay dividends annually, and receiving these payouts at strategically chosen times can enhance their utility. For instance, aligning dividend payments with financial planning milestones—such as funding educational expenses or making a significant purchase—can help policyholders make the most of their whole life insurance. Furthermore, understanding the historical performance of various mutual companies can inform decisions about when to adjust premium payments or take advantage of dividends to maximize overall returns.

Incorporating premium payments into a family financial legacy plan requires a thoughtful approach. Agents should work closely with clients to assess their long-term financial goals and the role that whole life insurance plays in achieving them. By developing a comprehensive strategy that includes regular premium assessments and adjustments, families can ensure that their policies remain effective tools for wealth transfer and estate planning. This ongoing evaluation process not only strengthens the family's financial foundation but also reinforces the importance of whole life insurance as a key component of their financial legacy.

Finally, the flexibility of whole life policies allows for adjustments in premium payments based on changing circumstances. Life events, such as the birth of a child or changes in employment, may necessitate a reevaluation of premium amounts. Agents should emphasize the importance of maintaining open communication with clients regarding their financial status and goals. By fostering this dialogue, agents can help clients navigate potential challenges and leverage their whole life insurance effectively, ensuring that it remains a vital part of their financial planning strategy, now and into the future.

Chapter 4: Comparing Mutual Companies

Key Players in the Market

The market for whole life insurance, particularly through mutual companies, is shaped by several key players that influence both the products available and the strategies employed by life insurance agents and customers alike. Mutual insurance companies, owned by policyholders rather than shareholders, are at the forefront, offering dividend whole life policies that allow individuals to build a financial banking system. These companies focus on long-term stability and sustainability, ensuring that policyholders not only receive death benefits but also accumulate cash value that can be leveraged for various financial needs.

Agents play a critical role in navigating this market. They serve as the bridge between clients and the array of products offered by mutual companies. A knowledgeable agent understands the intricacies of dividend payouts and can help clients strategize on how to maximize these benefits over time. This involves educating clients about the importance of policy performance, the historical dividend rates of different companies, and how to make informed decisions that align with their long-term financial goals. Their expertise is essential in guiding families to select policies that not only secure their financial future but also integrate seamlessly into their overall legacy planning.

The competitive landscape among mutual companies is another significant factor in the market. Each company has its unique approach to dividend whole life insurance, with varying policy features, premium structures, and dividend histories. By comparing these companies, agents and clients can identify which providers offer the best policies tailored to their specific financial situations. Analyzing the financial strength and historical performance of these companies is crucial for agents, as it enables them to recommend the most reliable options for clients looking to build their financial bank through whole life insurance.

Understanding the loan features of dividend whole life insurance is vital for both agents and customers. These features allow policyholders to access the cash value of their policies through loans, providing a flexible source of funding for emergencies, investments, or other financial needs. However, it is essential to comprehend the implications of borrowing against a policy, including how it affects the death benefit and the overall growth of cash value. Agents must effectively communicate these details to ensure clients make informed decisions that support their financial legacy without jeopardizing their long-term goals.

Lastly, the integration of whole life insurance into a family financial legacy plan highlights the significance of risk management. Whole life policies not only provide a death benefit but also serve as a stable financial resource that can help families navigate unexpected challenges. By leveraging the cash value, families can create emergency funds, fund retirement plans, or facilitate wealth transfer with minimized tax implications. Key players in this market, including agents and mutual companies, must work collaboratively to educate clients on the multifaceted benefits of whole life insurance, ultimately empowering them to craft a legacy that endures for generations.

Evaluating Dividend History

Evaluating the dividend history of a whole life insurance policy is essential for life insurance agents and infinite banking customers aiming to build a robust financial legacy. The dividend history offers critical insights into how a mutual company has performed financially over time. This historical performance can indicate the company's stability, reliability, and commitment to its policyholders. By reviewing past dividend payouts, agents can provide clients with a clearer picture of what to expect in terms of future returns, which is crucial for crafting a long-term financial plan.

When analyzing dividend history, it is important to consider the consistency of payouts. A company that has a track record of paying dividends regularly, even during economic downturns, demonstrates resilience and sound financial management. Clients should be encouraged to look for companies that have maintained or increased their dividend payouts over the years. This consistency can signify a strong financial foundation that supports the sustainable growth of cash value within the whole life policy, ultimately enhancing the financial banking system that clients aim to establish for their families.

Moreover, the rate of dividend increases can also be a telling factor in evaluating a mutual company's performance. A steady increase in dividends indicates not only profitability but also a commitment to sharing that success with policyholders. Life insurance agents should guide their clients in understanding the importance of this aspect, as it reflects the company's ability to generate surplus earnings and its willingness to distribute those earnings fairly. By selecting a company with a strong history of increasing dividends, clients can better position themselves for maximizing their returns and enhancing their financial legacy.

In addition to consistency and growth rates, agents should also assess how dividend histories correlate with overall company performance indicators such as asset growth, return on equity, and claims-paying ability. These factors together provide a comprehensive view of the mutual company's health and its capacity to support policyholders through dividends. Understanding these metrics can empower clients to make informed decisions about which policies align with their financial goals, especially in the context of estate planning and wealth transfer strategies.

Finally, it is beneficial for clients to engage in discussions about the implications of dividend history on their financial strategies. For instance, a strong dividend history not only boosts confidence in the policy but can also impact decisions regarding cash value utilization for emergencies or retirement funding. By leveraging this information, clients can craft a self-funding retirement plan that integrates whole life insurance as a cornerstone of their financial legacy, ensuring stability and security for generations to come.

Assessing Financial Strength and Ratings

Assessing the financial strength and ratings of mutual companies offering dividend whole life insurance is a crucial step for life insurance agents and infinite banking customers. When considering such policies, understanding the financial health of the insurer is paramount. Financial strength ratings, provided by independent rating agencies such as A.M. Best, Fitch, and Moody's, offer insights into the company's ability to meet its ongoing obligations to policyholders. These ratings reflect various factors, including the company's balance sheet, operational performance, and competitive position in the market, thereby enabling prospective policyholders to make informed decisions.

A strong financial rating indicates a mutual company's stability and reliability, which are essential when selecting a dividend whole life policy. Agents should emphasize the importance of choosing a company with a solid track record of paying dividends consistently to its policyholders. This consistency not only enhances the policy's cash value but also ensures that the family's financial legacy is bolstered over time. When agents present options to clients, they should highlight how a company's financial strength can directly impact the benefits received from the policy, including dividend payouts and overall cash accumulation.

Additionally, clients should be educated on the significance of mutual companies in the context of whole life insurance. Unlike stock companies, mutual companies are owned by policyholders, which means that profits are returned to them in the form of dividends. This ownership structure can contribute to a more favorable financial position for policyholders, as it aligns the interests of the company with those of its clients. Agents should assist clients in comparing the financial ratings and historical dividend performance of different mutual companies to identify options that align with their long-term financial goals.

Moreover, understanding the implications of financial strength on estate planning and wealth transfer is vital. A well-rated mutual company can provide policyholders with the confidence that their family's financial future is secure. Whole life insurance not only serves as a means of wealth accumulation but also as a tool for estate planning, allowing for a seamless transfer of assets to beneficiaries. Agents should illustrate how selecting a financially robust provider can enhance the effectiveness of wealth transfer strategies and ensure that the intended legacy is preserved.

Finally, leveraging cash value from whole life policies for emergencies or retirement planning underscores the importance of financial strength. A company's ability to provide loans against the cash value of a policy without jeopardizing its stability is a key consideration for clients. By assessing the financial ratings of mutual companies, agents can help clients understand the potential risks and benefits associated with borrowing against their policies. This understanding reinforces the role of whole life insurance as a crucial component of a comprehensive financial banking system that supports the needs of families both now and in the future.

Chapter 5: The Role of Whole Life Insurance in Estate Planning

Integrating Whole Life Insurance into Your Estate Plan

Integrating whole life insurance into your estate plan is a strategic move that can significantly enhance wealth transfer and provide financial security for future generations. Whole life insurance, particularly from mutual companies, offers a guaranteed death benefit, cash value accumulation, and dividends, making it a valuable tool in estate planning. By incorporating these policies into your financial legacy plan, you can ensure that your loved ones are not only protected but also positioned to benefit from a stable financial foundation that can support their needs for years to come.

One of the primary advantages of utilizing whole life insurance in estate planning is its ability to provide liquidity. Upon the policyholder's passing, the death benefit can be used to cover estate taxes, debts, and other financial obligations, preventing the need to liquidate other assets. This feature is especially crucial for individuals with significant illiquid assets, such as real estate or business interests, as it allows families to retain these assets without financial strain. By planning ahead with whole life insurance, you can facilitate a smoother transition of wealth and minimize the impact of taxes on your estate.

Maximizing dividend payouts is another critical aspect of integrating whole life insurance into an estate plan. Selecting policies from mutual companies known for their strong dividend performance can enhance the cash value growth of your policy, providing additional funds that can be accessed during your lifetime or passed on to heirs. Life insurance agents can play a vital role in advising clients on which mutual companies consistently deliver high dividend returns, allowing policyholders to make informed decisions that align with their financial goals.

In addition to death benefits and dividends, whole life insurance also offers the opportunity to leverage cash value for emergencies or additional investment opportunities. This feature can serve as a financial safety net, ensuring that your family has access to funds when needed. By strategically accessing the cash value through loans, policyholders can maintain their policy's death benefit while utilizing the funds for various purposes, such as college tuition, home purchases, or business investments. Such strategies not only enhance the financial legacy but also promote a culture of resourcefulness within the family.

When considering the integration of whole life insurance into your estate plan, it is essential to understand the unique characteristics of each policy and the potential tax benefits. Whole life insurance can provide tax-free death benefits to beneficiaries, and the cash value grows on a tax-deferred basis. These attributes make whole life insurance an attractive option for long-term savings and wealth preservation. By collaborating with financial advisors and estate planners, you can create a comprehensive financial strategy that aligns with your family's values and aspirations, ensuring that your legacy is not only preserved but also thrives for generations to come.

Wealth Transfer Strategies

Wealth transfer strategies are essential for individuals looking to create a lasting legacy for their families while ensuring financial stability. Whole life insurance from mutual companies serves as a cornerstone for these strategies, offering not only a death benefit but also a cash value component that can be leveraged during the policyholder's lifetime. By integrating whole life insurance into a broader financial plan, policyholders can effectively manage their wealth transfer, ensuring that their assets are preserved and passed on to future generations in a tax-efficient manner.

One of the primary advantages of whole life insurance is its ability to accumulate cash value over time, which can be utilized in various ways. Policyholders can borrow against this cash value for emergencies, investments, or other financial needs, allowing for flexibility that traditional savings accounts do not offer. This access to cash value provides a safety net, ensuring that families can cover unexpected expenses without depleting their savings or interrupting their long-term financial goals. The ability to leverage cash value aligns well with the concept of a self-funding retirement plan, where policyholders can utilize their whole life insurance as a reliable source of income during retirement.

When considering wealth transfer, the dividend payouts from whole life insurance policies play a crucial role. By selecting a mutual company with a strong track record of paying dividends, policyholders can increase the overall value of their policies, enhancing the financial resources available for future generations. Strategies for maximizing these dividend payouts include regular premium payments and maintaining the policy in good standing, which can result in higher returns over time. Understanding the nuances of how dividends are calculated and distributed can help life insurance agents provide valuable insights to their clients, ensuring they make informed decisions regarding their policies.

Estate planning is another critical aspect of wealth transfer strategies. Whole life insurance can provide liquidity needed to cover estate taxes, ensuring that heirs can inherit assets without the burden of immediate financial obligations. By integrating whole life insurance into an estate plan, families can create a seamless transition of wealth, preserving the family legacy while minimizing the impact of taxation. This approach not only safeguards the family's financial future but also reinforces the importance of financial education and planning for younger generations.

Ultimately, the success of a wealth transfer strategy hinges on understanding the unique features of whole life insurance and how they can be utilized effectively. Life insurance agents play a pivotal role in guiding clients through the intricacies of choosing the right policies, understanding loan features, and comparing mutual companies to find the best dividend whole life options. By fostering a comprehensive understanding of these elements, agents can empower clients to create robust financial banking systems that support their families and contribute to a sustainable legacy for years to come.

Utilizing Death Benefits for Estate Liquidity

Utilizing death benefits for estate liquidity is an essential strategy for ensuring that a family's financial obligations are met upon the passing of a loved one. Whole life insurance, particularly dividend-paying policies from mutual companies, serves as a reliable tool in this regard. The death benefit can provide immediate liquidity to cover various expenses, such as outstanding debts, funeral costs, and estate taxes. This financial security grants beneficiaries peace of mind, knowing that they will not be burdened with immediate financial pressures during a difficult time.

When strategically integrated into estate planning, the death benefit from whole life insurance can significantly enhance the overall financial stability of an estate. It allows for the smooth transfer of wealth without the need for liquidating other assets, which may not be timely or favorable. For instance, if a family business is part of the estate, the death benefit can help cover inheritance taxes, ensuring that the business remains intact and can continue to operate without disruption. This approach not only preserves family legacies but also supports the ongoing financial health of the remaining family members.

Life insurance agents play a critical role in guiding clients through the selection of the right whole life policy. By comparing dividend-paying whole life insurance products from various mutual companies, agents can assist clients in finding policies that offer competitive death benefits and favorable dividend payout histories. The choice of company can influence the size of the death benefit and the overall financial performance of the policy, making it vital for agents to have a thorough understanding of the options available in the market.

In addition to immediate liquidity, the cash value accumulated in whole life policies can also support estate liquidity strategies. Policyholders have the option to borrow against their cash value, providing an additional resource in times of need without disrupting the death benefit. This flexibility can be particularly useful for addressing unforeseen expenses that may arise during the estate settlement process. Utilizing the cash value in tandem with the death benefit enhances the financial framework, allowing families to manage their obligations effectively.

Ultimately, leveraging death benefits and cash value from whole life insurance policies creates a robust financial safety net for families. By incorporating these elements into a comprehensive estate plan, clients can ensure that their loved ones are financially protected and that their legacy is preserved. This strategic approach not only facilitates estate liquidity but also underscores the importance of whole life insurance as a foundational component of a family's financial legacy.

Chapter 6: Leveraging Cash Value from Whole Life Policies

Understanding Cash Value Accumulation

Understanding cash value accumulation is essential for life insurance agents and infinite banking customers who aim to leverage dividend whole life insurance from mutual companies as a foundational element of their financial strategy. Cash value in whole life insurance policies grows over time, offering a dual benefit: providing a death benefit to beneficiaries while also serving as a living asset that can be accessed during the policyholder's lifetime. This accumulation is typically facilitated through premium payments that are allocated not only to the death benefit but also to a cash value account that grows at a guaranteed rate, often bolstered by dividends declared by the mutual company.

The growth of cash value is influenced by several factors, including the policy's guaranteed interest rate and the dividends paid by the mutual company. The dividends are not guaranteed but are based on the company's performance, which can be affected by various economic conditions. When selecting a mutual company for a whole life insurance policy, it is crucial to analyze their historical dividend performance and financial stability. Agents and customers alike should focus on companies with a strong track record of consistent dividend payouts, as this can significantly enhance the cash value accumulation over time.

Maximizing cash value accumulation requires strategic planning. Policyholders can enhance their cash value growth by making additional premium payments or utilizing paid-up additions, which allow for the purchase of extra coverage that also contributes to cash value. This strategy not only accelerates cash value growth but leverages the power of compounding interest. Understanding how to effectively structure these payments and additions can provide a robust financial tool that supports both current needs and long-term objectives, such as retirement funding or emergency reserves.

Incorporating cash value from whole life policies into an overall financial legacy plan can provide a safety net for families. The cash value can be accessed through loans, providing liquidity without triggering taxable events. This feature makes whole life insurance an attractive option for emergency funds, allowing families to navigate unexpected expenses without disrupting their overall financial strategy. Additionally, the tax advantages associated with cash value growth and policy loans can enhance the financial benefits of using whole life insurance as part of a broader estate planning strategy.

Finally, understanding the interplay between cash value accumulation and risk management is vital. Whole life insurance can act as a stabilizing force for family finances, creating a secure foundation that can withstand economic uncertainties. By incorporating whole life insurance into a family financial legacy plan, individuals can ensure that their loved ones are protected while also building a sustainable financial resource. This dual purpose underscores the importance of cash value accumulation in achieving a comprehensive financial strategy that supports both immediate and long-term goals.

Utilizing Cash Value for Emergency Funds

Utilizing cash value from whole life insurance policies as an emergency fund is an innovative strategy that can provide financial security during unexpected events. Whole life insurance, particularly when sourced from mutual companies, accumulates cash value over time, allowing policyholders to access funds without the need for traditional loans or credit. This feature enables families to maintain liquidity while safeguarding their long-term financial goals. By understanding how to leverage this cash value effectively, life insurance agents can guide clients through the nuances of emergency funding, presenting it as a viable alternative to more conventional financial resources.

One of the key advantages of using cash value from whole life policies is the accessibility it offers. Unlike savings accounts or other investment vehicles that may impose penalties for early withdrawals, the cash value in a whole life insurance policy can be accessed through withdrawals or loans, often without incurring tax liabilities. This flexibility is crucial during emergencies, where immediate cash flow is necessary to cover unexpected expenses.

Agents should educate clients on how to utilize this feature responsibly, ensuring they understand the implications of loans on their policy's death benefit and overall financial health.

Maximizing dividend payouts is another essential aspect of using whole life insurance as an emergency fund. Dividend payments can contribute significantly to the cash value accumulation within a policy, enhancing the available funds for emergencies. Life insurance agents should emphasize the importance of selecting mutual companies known for their strong dividend performance, as this could lead to a more substantial buffer during financial crises. By comparing the dividend histories and payout structures of various mutual companies, agents can help clients make informed choices that align with their financial objectives.

Integrating cash value as an emergency fund within a broader financial strategy can also aid in effective estate planning and wealth transfer. Families can use the cash value to cover immediate financial needs, ensuring that other assets remain intact for inheritance purposes. This approach can prevent the forced liquidation of investments or properties during a financial emergency, preserving the family's wealth for future generations. Agents play a vital role in helping clients understand how this integration can enhance their overall financial legacy.

Finally, it is essential to discuss the strategic planning involved in using cash value for emergencies. While the immediate benefits are clear, policyholders should be counseled on maintaining a balance between accessing cash value and ensuring the policy remains in force. Understanding the loan features of dividend whole life insurance is crucial, as improper management could lead to unintended consequences, such as reduced death benefits or policy lapse. By fostering a comprehensive understanding of these elements, life insurance agents can empower clients to utilize their whole life insurance policies effectively, ensuring they are well-prepared for both planned and unplanned financial challenges.

Impact of Withdrawals on Policy Health

Withdrawals from dividend whole life insurance policies can significantly impact the overall health of a family's financial strategy. When policyholders withdraw funds from their cash value, they are essentially reducing the amount of money that can generate future dividends. This reduction can lead to a decrease in the policy's overall performance, as dividends are typically calculated based on the remaining cash value. Therefore, it is essential for policyholders to weigh the short-term benefits of immediate access to cash against the long-term implications for their policy's growth and financial legacy.

The careful management of withdrawals is crucial for maximizing dividend payouts. Policyholders must understand that while accessing cash value can provide liquidity in times of need, it can also diminish the compounding effect of their policy. Each withdrawal not only reduces the cash value but can also lower future dividend earnings, which can impact the policy's performance over time. Consequently, agents should educate clients on the importance of strategic withdrawals and encourage them to consider alternatives, such as policy loans, which may allow them to access funds without interrupting the compounding growth of their cash value.

Comparing mutual companies is essential when evaluating the impact of withdrawals on policy health. Not all mutual companies structure their policies the same way, and the terms regarding withdrawals can vary significantly. Some companies may offer more favorable terms, including higher dividend payouts and lower costs associated with withdrawals. It is vital for both agents and clients to conduct thorough research to identify which mutual companies provide the best dividend whole life policies, as this can influence long-term financial outcomes and the stability of a family's financial banking system.

Whole life insurance plays a prominent role in estate planning and wealth transfer, and the management of withdrawals can directly affect these goals. When funds are withdrawn, the remaining death benefit may also be impacted, potentially leaving heirs with less than anticipated. Families looking to create a lasting financial legacy should approach withdrawals with caution, ensuring that they maintain sufficient cash value to uphold the policy's function as a wealth transfer tool. Life insurance agents should guide clients in making informed decisions about withdrawals, emphasizing the importance of maintaining a balance between immediate needs and long-term objectives.

Incorporating dividend whole life insurance into a family's financial legacy plan requires a comprehensive understanding of how withdrawals affect policy health. By leveraging cash value responsibly and being aware of the potential consequences of withdrawals, families can create a sustainable financial framework that supports their long-term goals. Policyholders should be encouraged to regularly review their financial strategies with their agents, ensuring that their approach to withdrawals aligns with their broader financial aspirations and enables them to build a robust legacy for future generations.

Chapter 7: Tax Benefits of Dividend Whole Life Insurance

Tax-Deferred Growth of Cash Value

Tax-deferred growth of cash value in dividend whole life insurance is a critical component that agents and customers alike must understand when integrating this financial tool into their broader financial strategies. Unlike traditional investment vehicles, the cash value accumulated in a whole life policy grows on a tax-deferred basis. This means that policyholders can watch their investments compound over time without the immediate tax implications that accompany many other investment options. By leveraging this feature, families can enhance their long-term savings and create a more stable financial foundation.

The tax-deferred growth mechanism is particularly advantageous for those who are building a financial system to support their families. As the cash value of a whole life policy increases, it offers policyholders a unique opportunity to access funds without incurring tax liabilities. This liquidity can be essential in times of need, allowing families to navigate emergencies or seize investment opportunities while preserving their overall wealth. Understanding how to utilize this cash value effectively is paramount for agents advising clients on how to maximize the benefits of their policies.

Moreover, the tax benefits associated with whole life insurance extend beyond just the growth of cash value. When policyholders eventually withdraw or take loans against their cash value, they can do so without facing income tax, provided the policy remains in force. This feature allows for a strategic approach to managing cash flow, enabling families to utilize their funds without the usual tax burdens. Agents can play a vital role in guiding clients through these options, ensuring they make informed decisions that align with their financial goals.

In the context of estate planning and wealth transfer, the tax-deferred growth of cash value serves as a powerful tool. Families can build a legacy that not only provides for their immediate needs but also ensures that future generations benefit from their financial foresight. By integrating whole life insurance into an estate plan, individuals can create a tax-efficient way to pass on wealth while simultaneously growing their assets. Agents who understand the nuances of this strategy can effectively communicate its value to clients looking to establish a lasting family legacy.

Ultimately, maximizing the potential of tax-deferred growth requires a comprehensive understanding of the features and benefits of dividend whole life insurance. Agents must stay informed about the various mutual companies and their respective policies to recommend the best options for their clients. This knowledge enables them to provide tailored advice that aligns with the specific needs and goals of each family, ensuring that the financial banking system they create is robust and sustainable. By emphasizing the importance of tax-deferred cash value growth, agents can empower their clients to build a solid financial foundation that supports their family's legacy for generations to come.

Tax-Free Death Benefit

Tax-free death benefits are a cornerstone of whole life insurance policies, particularly those offered by mutual companies. For life insurance agents and infinite banking customers, understanding how these benefits operate is essential for effective financial planning. When a policyholder passes away, the death benefit is paid out to the designated beneficiaries without being subject to federal income taxes. This tax advantage not only provides immediate financial support to surviving family members but also plays a crucial role in wealth transfer strategies within estate planning.

In the context of building a family legacy, the tax-free nature of these benefits becomes even more significant. By leveraging whole life insurance, families can ensure that their loved ones receive a financial cushion during a challenging time, while also preserving the wealth accumulated over generations. This assurance allows policyholders to create a more comprehensive financial strategy that accounts for potential estate taxes and other liabilities that could erode their family's wealth. The death benefit acts as a protective measure against these financial pitfalls, enabling a smoother transition of assets to the next generation.

When comparing mutual companies and their dividend whole life policies, it is critical to assess not only the premium rates and growth potential but also the death benefit structure. Some companies may offer more favorable terms than others regarding the distribution and growth of dividends, which can further enhance the overall value of the policy. Agents should guide clients in selecting a mutual company that aligns with their long-term goals, ensuring that the death benefit remains a robust feature of their financial banking system.

Additionally, the tax-free death benefit complements the financial strategies associated with cash value accumulation. As policyholders build cash value throughout the life of their insurance policy, they can utilize this resource for emergencies or investment opportunities without jeopardizing the future death benefit. This dual functionality allows families to tap into their policy's growth while safeguarding their legacy. Agents can educate clients on how to balance the use of cash value and the preservation of the death benefit to optimize their financial stability.

Incorporating tax-free death benefits into a broader financial legacy plan ultimately enhances risk management strategies for families. With the assurance that their loved ones will receive a significant tax-free payout, policyholders can focus on other aspects of their financial health, such as retirement planning and emergency funding. This integrated approach not only builds a robust financial foundation but also fosters peace of mind, knowing that their family's financial future is secure, regardless of life's uncertainties.

Tax Implications of Policy Loans

Tax implications of policy loans are a critical consideration for both life insurance agents and infinite banking customers when leveraging dividend whole life insurance. When policyholders borrow against the cash value of their whole life policies, they do so without triggering a taxable event, provided the policy remains in force. This unique feature of whole life insurance allows individuals to access funds for various needs—such as emergencies, investments, or family expenses—while deferring any tax liabilities. The ability to take loans against the policy creates a powerful financial tool, enabling policyholders to maintain liquidity without sacrificing the tax advantages associated with their insurance.

It's essential to understand that while policy loans are tax-free, they are not without consequences. If the loan is not repaid, the outstanding balance, including interest, will be deducted from the death benefit. This reduction can have significant implications for estate planning and wealth transfer strategies, as heirs may receive less than expected. Therefore, policyholders must be strategic in their borrowing practices, ensuring that they develop a plan for repayment to preserve the intended financial legacy for their families.

Another important aspect of policy loans is the potential impact on the policy's cash value and dividend payouts. When a loan is taken, the insurer typically calculates dividends on the remaining cash value, which is the total cash value minus the loan amount. This can lead to a reduction in dividends if a substantial loan is outstanding. For those focused on maximizing dividend payouts, it's prudent to assess how borrowing against the cash value can affect overall returns and to adjust their financial strategy accordingly.

The relationship between policy loans and tax implications also extends to how these loans can be utilized in retirement planning. As individuals approach retirement, accessing cash value through loans provides a way to supplement income without incurring immediate tax liabilities. However, careful planning is necessary to ensure that the policy remains viable throughout retirement. If the policy lapses due to unpaid loans, it could result in taxable income equal to the unpaid loan amount, creating an unexpected financial burden.

In conclusion, understanding the tax implications of policy loans is vital for life insurance agents and infinite banking customers alike. By leveraging the unique features of dividend whole life insurance, individuals can create a sustainable financial banking system that supports their family's needs while minimizing tax exposure. A well-crafted strategy that incorporates loan repayment, dividend maximization, and careful planning for estate transfer can enhance the benefits of whole life insurance, ensuring that it serves as a robust foundation for long-term wealth and financial security.

Chapter 8: Integrating Whole Life Insurance into a Family Financial Legacy Plan

Defining Your Family Legacy Goals

Defining your family legacy goals is an essential first step in crafting a comprehensive financial plan that incorporates whole life insurance. It requires you to articulate what you want your family legacy to embody, whether that means ensuring financial security, fostering education and entrepreneurial endeavors, or leaving a lasting philanthropic impact. By identifying these goals, you create a roadmap that guides not only your financial decisions but also the way you utilize financial tools like dividend whole life insurance from mutual companies. This approach facilitates a deeper understanding of how your choices today can shape your family's future.

When considering your family legacy goals, it is important to involve all stakeholders. Engage family members in discussions about values, aspirations, and the importance of financial literacy and stability. This collaborative approach ensures that everyone is on the same page and understands the purpose behind the financial strategies you implement. By aligning your family's vision with the benefits of whole life insurance, including its cash value growth and dividend payouts, you create a unified front that enhances your financial legacy.

Another critical aspect to consider is the long-term nature of whole life insurance. Unlike term policies, which provide temporary coverage, whole life insurance builds cash value over time, offering opportunities for leveraging funds for emergencies, educational expenses, or investments. As your family legacy goals evolve, the cash value can serve as a financial reservoir, enabling you to adapt your strategy to meet new challenges and opportunities. Understanding how to maximize dividend payouts and the tax benefits associated with these policies can further enhance your ability to achieve your legacy objectives.

Moreover, integrating whole life insurance into your family financial legacy plan also involves considering the role of estate planning and wealth transfer. Whole life policies can be instrumental in ensuring a smooth transition of assets to the next generation. By designating beneficiaries and understanding the implications of policy loans, you can navigate the complexities of wealth transfer while minimizing tax burdens. This foresight allows you to maintain your family's financial stability and ensure that your legacy goals are not only met but sustained over generations.

Ultimately, defining your family legacy goals is about more than just financial gain; it is about creating a lasting impact. As you explore the various ways to incorporate dividend whole life insurance into your financial plan, remember that the choices you make today will reverberate through your family for years to come. By prioritizing your legacy goals, involving family members in the process, and taking advantage of the multifaceted benefits of whole life insurance, you can build a robust financial banking system that not only supports your family but also serves as a testament to your values and aspirations.

Aligning Whole Life Policies with Legacy Objectives

Aligning whole life policies with legacy objectives is essential for those aiming to create a lasting financial impact for future generations. Whole life insurance, particularly from mutual companies, offers a unique combination of permanent coverage, cash value accumulation, and dividend payouts. These features not only serve to protect against unforeseen circumstances but also provide a reliable financial tool that can enhance estate planning and wealth transfer strategies. By understanding how to effectively align these policies with legacy goals, life insurance agents and infinite banking customers can facilitate a more secure financial future for their families.

To begin with, the cash value component of whole life insurance plays a pivotal role in achieving legacy objectives. As policyholders accumulate cash value over time, they can leverage this asset for various purposes, such as funding education, supporting entrepreneurial ventures, or providing emergency funds for unexpected expenses. By strategically utilizing the cash value, families can create a self-sustaining banking system that supports ongoing financial needs while simultaneously laying the groundwork for a robust legacy. This alignment ensures that whole life policies not only serve immediate financial needs but also contribute to long-term family wealth.

Maximizing dividend payouts is another critical aspect of aligning whole life policies with legacy objectives. Agents can guide clients in selecting mutual companies known for their competitive dividend rates, thereby enhancing the policy's overall performance. By understanding the intricacies of dividend calculations and the factors influencing payouts, policyholders can make informed decisions that maximize returns over time. This approach not only strengthens the financial foundation of the policy but also ensures that the benefits can be passed down through generations, reinforcing the family's legacy.

Furthermore, integrating whole life insurance into a comprehensive family financial legacy plan requires careful consideration of estate planning and wealth transfer strategies. Whole life policies can serve as a powerful tool for mitigating estate taxes, ensuring that more of the family's wealth is preserved for heirs. Additionally, designating beneficiaries and considering trust arrangements can provide further layers of protection and control over wealth distribution. Life insurance agents play a crucial role in educating clients about these strategies, thereby facilitating a seamless transition of assets and reinforcing the family's financial legacy.

In conclusion, aligning whole life policies with legacy objectives is a multifaceted process that encompasses cash value utilization, dividend maximization, and strategic estate planning. By embracing these elements, life insurance agents and infinite banking customers can harness the full potential of whole life insurance as a foundational component of a family legacy. Through informed decision-making and proactive planning, they can create a financial framework that not only protects their loved ones but also enriches future generations, ultimately fulfilling their legacy aspirations.

Communication and Education for Family Members

Effective communication and education for family members are essential components when integrating whole life insurance into a family's financial plan. For life insurance agents and infinite banking customers, understanding the nuances of whole life insurance, particularly with mutual companies, is crucial in ensuring that all family members are well-informed about the benefits and strategies associated with these policies. Clear communication helps demystify the complexities of dividend whole life insurance and encourages proactive engagement in financial planning, ultimately leading to a more cohesive family legacy.

An integral aspect of this communication is the need to explain the mechanics of how whole life insurance operates, particularly in regards to cash value and dividends. Families should grasp the significance of the cash value component, which grows over time, and understand how dividends can be utilized to further enhance their financial positions. Providing family members with accessible resources and educational materials can foster discussions that lead to a deeper understanding of how dividend payouts can impact their long-term savings and overall wealth accumulation.

Moreover, family education sessions can focus on comparing different mutual companies to identify which offers the most advantageous dividend whole life policies. This comparative analysis can empower families to make informed decisions that align with their financial goals. Engaging family members in discussions about the features and benefits of various policies can also encourage them to take an active role in their financial planning, promoting a sense of ownership and responsibility for their family's financial future.

The role of whole life insurance in estate planning and wealth transfer is another critical area for discussion. Families need to understand how these policies can serve as tools for passing down wealth while minimizing tax implications. Educating family members about the tax benefits associated with dividend whole life insurance for long-term savings can further solidify the importance of these policies within the family's financial strategy. Awareness of how these products function within the broader context of estate planning can lead to more thoughtful discussions about legacy and wealth transfer.

Finally, leveraging cash value from whole life policies for emergency funds and other financial needs should be a key topic in family education. By outlining the loan features of dividend whole life insurance, families can better appreciate how these policies can serve as a self-funding retirement plan, providing security and stability in times of need. The more family members understand the risk management benefits that whole life insurance offers, the more empowered they will feel to utilize these tools effectively, ultimately ensuring that their family legacy is both preserved and enhanced.

Chapter 9: Understanding the Loan Features of Dividend Whole Life Insurance

How Policy Loans Work

Policy loans from whole life insurance policies provide a unique opportunity for policyholders to access their cash value without triggering a taxable event. When a policyholder takes out a loan against their whole life insurance, they are essentially borrowing against the cash value that has accumulated in the policy. This cash value grows over time through a combination of premium payments, dividends, and guaranteed interest. The flexibility of policy loans allows individuals to utilize their policy as a financial resource, offering liquidity that can be used for various financial needs, such as funding an emergency, making investments, or supporting family expenses.

The mechanics of how policy loans work are straightforward. Once a policyholder has built sufficient cash value, they can request a loan from their insurance company. The amount available for borrowing is typically a percentage of the cash value, and the policyholder does not need to undergo a credit check, as the loan is secured by the policy itself. Interest rates on these loans are generally lower than traditional loans, and the terms are flexible. The loan does not require monthly payments; however, unpaid interest will accumulate and be added to the loan balance. This structure allows policyholders to manage their cash flow while benefiting from the underlying life insurance coverage.

One of the key advantages of policy loans is that they do not reduce the death benefit of the policy unless the loan is not repaid. This means that the policyholder can access funds while still ensuring the financial security of their beneficiaries. Additionally, if the policyholder passes away with an outstanding loan, the death benefit will be reduced by the loan amount, but the remaining funds will still provide a legacy for the family. This feature makes policy loans an attractive option for individuals looking to balance their immediate financial needs with long-term planning for their heirs.

Policy loans can also play a crucial role in a broader financial strategy, particularly in the context of infinite banking. By treating the whole life policy as a personal banking system, policyholders can leverage the cash value efficiently. This method allows them to take loans for investments or other opportunities while allowing the cash value to continue growing, driven by the policy's dividends and interest. This dual benefit of accessing cash while maintaining growth potential is an essential aspect of integrating whole life insurance into a family financial legacy plan.

In conclusion, understanding how policy loans work is vital for life insurance agents and infinite banking customers alike. By exploring the intricacies of borrowing against whole life insurance, individuals can make informed decisions that align with their financial goals. Whether it's for emergency funds, investment opportunities, or estate planning, the strategic use of policy loans provides a valuable tool for enhancing personal and family financial stability. With the right approach, policy loans can significantly contribute to building a sustainable financial legacy that supports future generations.

Advantages and Disadvantages of Borrowing

Borrowing against the cash value of dividend whole life insurance policies can offer several advantages that make it an attractive financial strategy for families. One of the primary benefits is the accessibility of funds. Policyholders can tap into the cash value without undergoing lengthy approval processes typical of traditional loans. This ease of access provides flexibility, allowing families to address emergencies, invest in opportunities, or cover unexpected expenses promptly. Moreover, the interest rates on loans against whole life policies are often lower than those of conventional loans, making this an economical option for borrowing.

Another significant advantage of borrowing from a whole life policy is the potential for continued growth of the cash value. When policyholders take a loan, their remaining cash value continues to accumulate dividends and interest, which is not the case with most traditional loans where the borrowed amount ceases to grow. This unique characteristic allows families to leverage their policy effectively, benefiting from both the loan and the ongoing growth of their investment. Additionally, since the loan does not require repayment during the policyholder's lifetime, it provides a sense of financial security and reduces the pressure to meet monthly payment obligations.

However, it is crucial to consider the disadvantages associated with borrowing against whole life insurance. One major concern is the impact on the death benefit. If the loan is not repaid, the outstanding amount plus interest will be deducted from the death benefit payable to beneficiaries. This reduction in the death benefit can affect the financial legacy intended for loved ones, making it essential for families to have a clear repayment strategy. Furthermore, excessive borrowing can lead to policy lapses if the cash value diminishes significantly, potentially resulting in loss of coverage and financial stability.

Another disadvantage worth noting is the interest charged on the borrowed amount. While rates may be lower than conventional loans, they still represent a cost that needs to be managed. If the borrowed funds are not utilized effectively, the potential for negative returns increases, impacting the overall financial plan. It is important for policyholders to weigh the benefits of access to cash against the costs associated with borrowing, ensuring that their financial strategy remains sound and sustainable.

In conclusion, borrowing against dividend whole life insurance presents a blend of advantages and disadvantages that must be carefully evaluated. For life insurance agents and infinite banking customers, understanding these dynamics is essential for crafting a robust financial legacy. By leveraging the benefits while mitigating the risks, families can create a financial banking system that supports their long-term goals and enhances their overall wealth strategy. Ultimately, informed decision-making regarding borrowing can lead to a more secure financial future, preserving the legacy intended for future generations.

Repayment Strategies

Repayment strategies for loans taken against dividend whole life insurance policies are crucial for maintaining the integrity of your financial banking system. When utilizing the cash value of a whole life policy, it is essential to understand that while loans can provide immediate liquidity, they also come with the obligation of repayment. The first strategy involves prioritizing repayments to prevent the accumulation of interest and potential reduction of death benefits. By making consistent payments, policyholders can ensure that their financial legacy remains intact and that their beneficiaries receive the full intended amount upon their passing.

Another effective strategy is to utilize the dividends generated by the whole life policy to assist in loan repayments. Many mutual companies offer policies with strong dividend performance, enabling policyholders to reinvest these dividends directly into their loan balances. This not only reduces the principal owed but also gives policyholders the advantage of compounding growth in their remaining cash value. It is important to regularly review dividend performance and adjust repayment strategies accordingly, ensuring that the approach remains aligned with the financial goals of the family.

Policyholders should also consider a structured repayment plan that aligns with their overall financial strategy. This can involve scheduling repayments in a way that coincides with income streams or other financial obligations, thus minimizing the strain on household finances. By creating a repayment timeline that fits within a broader financial plan, individuals can manage cash flow more effectively while still benefiting from the flexibility that whole life insurance offers. This strategic planning can lead to a more sustainable approach to utilizing the cash value of the policy.

Understanding the loan features of dividend whole life insurance is another vital aspect of repayment strategies. Different mutual companies may have varying terms regarding interest rates, repayment periods, and the impact on policy performance. Policyholders should take the time to review these features in detail to select a policy that provides favorable loan terms. This understanding can guide decision-making and help emphasize the importance of repaying loans in a timely manner to avoid adverse effects on the policy's cash value and death benefit.

Lastly, it is essential to communicate the importance of repayment strategies within the family. Engaging family members in discussions about the financial legacy and the role of whole life insurance can foster a collective understanding of the importance of maintaining the policy's health. By educating family members on how to leverage the policy for emergencies or opportunities while stressing the necessity of repayment, families can create a culture of financial responsibility that supports the longevity of their wealth-building efforts through whole life insurance.

Chapter 10: Building a Self-Funding Retirement Plan

Utilizing Whole Life Insurance for Retirement Income

Utilizing whole life insurance for retirement income offers a unique approach to financial planning that aligns closely with the principles of infinite banking. Whole life policies, particularly those issued by mutual companies, accumulate cash value over time, allowing policyholders to access funds during retirement. This feature provides a safety net that can be tapped into for various needs, including supplementing retirement income, funding emergencies, or even supporting lifestyle choices. By viewing whole life insurance not just as a death benefit but as a living asset, clients can leverage its cash value to create a robust financial foundation for their retirement years.

The strategy of maximizing dividend payouts in whole life insurance is crucial for enhancing retirement income. Policyholders can benefit from annual dividends, which can be reinvested to increase the cash value of the policy or taken as income during retirement. Understanding the nuances of how dividends are calculated and distributed by different mutual companies can significantly impact the overall returns. Life insurance agents can guide clients in selecting policies that not only provide reliable dividends but also align with their long-term financial goals, ensuring that their retirement income strategy is as robust as possible.

When comparing mutual companies, agents must focus on which ones offer the best dividend whole life policies. Factors such as company history, financial strength, and dividend performance should be taken into account. Clients should be encouraged to conduct thorough research or rely on expert advice to identify companies that have a consistent track record of strong performance and favorable dividend payouts. The right choice can lead to enhanced cash value accumulation and more substantial retirement income, reinforcing the importance of careful selection in the financial planning process.

Integrating whole life insurance into a family financial legacy plan positions it as a powerful tool for estate planning and wealth transfer. Policies can provide liquidity to cover estate taxes and other expenses, ensuring that family assets are preserved for future generations. Furthermore, the cash value of whole life insurance can serve as an emergency fund, allowing families to navigate financial challenges without depleting other resources. By incorporating whole life policies into their overall estate strategy, families can create a lasting legacy that supports their financial goals while providing stability and security.

The tax benefits of using dividend whole life insurance for long-term savings further enhance its appeal as a retirement income strategy. The cash value grows on a tax-deferred basis, and policyholders can access funds through loans or withdrawals without incurring immediate tax liabilities. This feature, combined with a well-structured financial plan, allows clients to enjoy the benefits of their whole life insurance policies while minimizing tax exposure. By understanding and effectively utilizing these advantages, individuals can build a self-funding retirement plan that not only meets their needs but also fortifies their family's financial future.

Creating a Sustainable Withdrawal Strategy

Creating a Sustainable Withdrawal Strategy involves a careful balance between accessing the cash value of dividend whole life insurance policies and ensuring the longevity of these funds for future use. For life insurance agents and infinite banking customers, understanding how to withdraw funds sustainably is crucial for maintaining the integrity of the financial system they have built. A well-crafted withdrawal strategy allows policyholders to utilize their cash value effectively while preserving the long-term benefits of their whole life insurance investment.

One of the key components of a sustainable withdrawal strategy is determining the optimal withdrawal amount. This requires an understanding of the policy's growth trajectory, including the impact of dividends on the cash value. Agents should educate clients about the importance of monitoring their policy performance and adjusting withdrawal amounts accordingly. A conservative approach, typically withdrawing a percentage of the cash value rather than a fixed dollar amount, can help ensure that the policy remains funded and continues to grow over time.

Additionally, agents and customers should consider the timing of withdrawals. Aligning withdrawals with specific financial goals, such as funding education or retirement, can enhance the overall effectiveness of the strategy. Understanding the loan features of dividend whole life insurance is essential, as borrowing against the cash value can sometimes provide a more advantageous solution than direct withdrawals. This method allows policyholders to access funds without incurring immediate tax consequences, preserving the policy's cash value for future growth.

Incorporating a comprehensive financial plan is also vital when creating a sustainable withdrawal strategy. By integrating whole life insurance into a family financial legacy plan, policyholders can ensure that their withdrawals align with broader financial objectives. This holistic approach allows for better risk management and enhances the policy's role in estate planning and wealth transfer. Life insurance agents should emphasize the importance of viewing the policy not just as a source of cash but as a foundational element of a family's financial stability.

Finally, continuous education and communication between agents and clients are paramount in maintaining a sustainable withdrawal strategy. Regular reviews of the policy's performance, the overall financial landscape, and changing family needs can help adjust withdrawal strategies as necessary. By fostering an ongoing dialogue, agents can better support their clients in leveraging their whole life insurance policies as a robust financial banking system, ultimately ensuring that these assets serve the family for generations to come.

Balancing Policy Growth and Retirement Needs

Balancing policy growth and retirement needs is a critical aspect for life insurance agents and infinite banking customers. As clients seek to secure their financial futures, understanding how dividend whole life insurance from mutual companies functions is essential. This type of insurance not only serves as a safety net but also acts as a powerful financial tool, allowing policyholders to access cash value while ensuring their families' long-term stability. Life insurance agents must educate clients on the dual benefits of policy growth and retirement readiness, demonstrating how these features can coexist harmoniously within a comprehensive financial plan.

One of the key strategies for maximizing dividend payouts involves selecting the right mutual company. Agents should guide their clients through a comparison of various mutual companies, focusing on their historical performance regarding dividends, financial strength, and customer service. By choosing a company with a solid track record, clients can enhance their policy growth potential. Additionally, understanding the nuances of each company's dividend declaration process can help clients make informed decisions, ensuring that their policies not only grow but also support their retirement needs effectively.

Integrating whole life insurance into a family financial legacy plan is another crucial consideration. Whole life policies provide a reliable source of cash value that can be leveraged for emergencies, education, or even retirement funding. Agents should emphasize how these policies can serve as a foundation for a self-funding retirement plan. Clients can borrow against their cash value to supplement their retirement income while allowing the policy to continue growing, thus striking a balance between immediate financial needs and long-term growth objectives.

The tax benefits of dividend whole life insurance further contribute to its role in balancing policy growth with retirement needs. The cash value growth in these policies is tax-deferred, and when structured correctly, policy loans can be taken without triggering tax liabilities. This feature allows clients to access funds while minimizing their tax burden, making whole life insurance a powerful tool in estate planning and wealth transfer. Agents should ensure that clients are aware of these advantages, as they can significantly impact financial strategies and retirement planning.

Finally, understanding the loan features of dividend whole life insurance is vital for managing both growth and retirement objectives. Policyholders can access their cash value through loans, providing liquidity without sacrificing the policy's death benefit. This flexibility enables clients to navigate life's uncertainties while maintaining their investment in the policy. Life insurance agents should work closely with clients to develop strategies that utilize these loan features effectively, ensuring that both policy growth and retirement needs are adequately addressed, leading to a stable financial future for families.

Chapter 11: Risk Management with Whole Life Insurance

Stabilizing Family Finances During Uncertain Times

Stabilizing family finances during uncertain times requires a comprehensive approach that incorporates reliable financial instruments. Dividend whole life insurance from mutual companies offers a unique solution, providing a safety net while simultaneously building cash value. As life insurance agents and infinite banking customers navigate these unpredictable environments, recognizing the stability that whole life insurance can offer is paramount. The guaranteed cash value growth and dividend payouts can create a buffer against financial instability, empowering families to weather economic storms without sacrificing their long-term financial goals.

Effective strategies for maximizing dividend payouts are essential for enhancing the benefits of whole life insurance. By working with mutual companies that have a track record of strong dividend performance, families can ensure that their policies are working as efficiently as possible. This includes selecting companies with robust financial health and a history of consistent dividend payments. Additionally, policyholders can engage in strategies such as paid-up additions, which increase both the cash value and the death benefit of the policy, thereby amplifying the impact of their investments during turbulent times.

When comparing mutual companies, it is crucial to analyze not only the dividend rates but also the overall policy structure and benefits. Some companies may offer higher dividends but come with higher fees or less favorable loan provisions. A thorough understanding of these variables will allow agents to recommend the most advantageous policies to their clients. By focusing on companies that prioritize policyholder interests and demonstrate a commitment to sustainable growth, families can establish a financial foundation that remains resilient in the face of uncertainty.

Whole life insurance plays a significant role in estate planning and wealth transfer, further stabilizing family finances. By incorporating whole life policies into a comprehensive estate plan, families can ensure that their assets are effectively transferred to the next generation, minimizing tax burdens and avoiding probate complications. The cash value accumulated in these policies can provide liquidity for heirs, allowing them to manage estate-related expenses without dipping into other investments or savings.

Leveraging cash value from whole life policies can also serve as an emergency fund during times of financial distress. Unlike traditional savings accounts, the cash value in a whole life insurance policy can be accessed through loans or withdrawals, providing immediate funds when needed. This flexibility is instrumental in maintaining financial stability, allowing families to address emergencies without resorting to high-interest debt options. Additionally, the tax benefits associated with accessing cash value further enhance the appeal of whole life insurance as a cornerstone of a family's financial legacy.

Whole Life Insurance as a Safety Net

Whole life insurance serves as a crucial safety net for families, providing both financial security and peace of mind in times of uncertainty. As a life insurance agent or an infinite banking customer, understanding the multifaceted benefits of whole life insurance can significantly enhance the financial stability of your clients or your own family. This type of insurance not only offers a death benefit but also accumulates cash value over time, which can be leveraged for various financial needs. When structured correctly, whole life insurance can act as a foundational element in a family's financial legacy, ensuring that loved ones are protected and that financial resources are available during emergencies.

One of the key advantages of whole life insurance is its predictable growth through dividends provided by mutual companies. These dividends can be reinvested into the policy to enhance cash value or used to purchase additional coverage. This strategy not only maximizes the overall benefit of the policy but also creates a robust financial tool that can be utilized in times of need. By comparing mutual companies, agents can guide clients in selecting policies that offer the best dividend rates, ensuring that families are not only protected but are also building wealth over time. The emphasis on dividend whole life policies creates a sustainable financial ecosystem that supports the policyholder's long-term goals.

Incorporating whole life insurance into estate planning is another essential aspect of creating a safety net for families. The cash value can be a powerful resource for wealth transfer, assisting in the management of estate taxes and ensuring that heirs receive their intended inheritance without financial burdens. By understanding the role of whole life insurance in estate planning, agents can help clients craft a comprehensive strategy that secures their family's future. This approach not only provides immediate financial protection but also lays the groundwork for generational wealth, highlighting the importance of long-term planning in financial discussions.

Leveraging the cash value of whole life insurance for emergency funds is a practical strategy that provides families with immediate access to liquidity when unexpected expenses arise. This feature allows policyholders to avoid high-interest debt options, promoting financial stability even in challenging times. Agents should educate clients about the loan features of dividend whole life policies, emphasizing how these loans can be repaid on flexible terms without jeopardizing the overall health of the policy. By integrating this strategy into a family's financial plan, whole life insurance becomes a dynamic tool that supports both current needs and future aspirations.

Finally, the tax benefits associated with dividend whole life insurance further solidify its role as a safety net. The cash value grows tax-deferred, and policyholders can access funds through loans without triggering taxable events. This unique characteristic positions whole life insurance as an effective long-term savings vehicle, enhancing its appeal for families looking to create a lasting financial legacy. By understanding and utilizing these tax advantages, agents and clients can craft a holistic financial plan that not only safeguards against risks but also promotes ongoing wealth accumulation, ensuring that the family legacy is preserved for generations to come.

Long-term Financial Resilience

Long-term financial resilience is a crucial aspect of personal and family financial planning, particularly when utilizing dividend whole life insurance from mutual companies. This financial tool not only provides a safety net for unexpected expenses but also plays a pivotal role in building a sustainable banking system that can support families for generations. By harnessing the guaranteed death benefit and the cash value accumulation of whole life policies, families can create a robust financial foundation that withstands economic fluctuations and personal financial crises.

To maximize the benefits of dividend whole life insurance, it is essential to understand the strategies that enhance dividend payouts. Policyholders need to recognize the significance of selecting a mutual company known for its strong financial performance and consistent dividend history. Agents should educate clients on how to effectively structure their policies and make informed decisions regarding premium payments and policy loans, which can significantly impact the long-term growth of cash value. By prioritizing these strategies, families can ensure their financial systems are resilient and capable of adapting to changing circumstances.

When comparing mutual companies for the best dividend whole life policies, agents must consider various factors beyond just the dividend rates. The overall financial health of the company, its claims-paying ability, and customer service reputation are critical components that influence long-term satisfaction and success. By providing clients with detailed analyses of different mutual companies, agents can guide them to make informed choices that align with their financial goals and legacy aspirations. This thorough evaluation process is vital in establishing a lasting financial legacy that supports family values and objectives.

Whole life insurance also plays a significant role in estate planning and wealth transfer, ensuring that family assets are preserved and passed on effectively. By integrating whole life policies into a comprehensive estate plan, families can mitigate tax liabilities and avoid potential probate issues. The cash value of these policies can be leveraged as a source of emergency funds or used to cover estate taxes, thereby preserving the family wealth for future generations. Agents should emphasize the importance of this strategic integration to enhance their clients' long-term financial resilience.

Ultimately, building a self-funding retirement plan with whole life insurance adds another layer of financial security. By utilizing the cash value for retirement income or as collateral for loans, policyholders can maintain their lifestyle without depleting their savings. Additionally, the risk management aspect of whole life insurance stabilizes family finances by providing a guaranteed death benefit that can protect against unforeseen circumstances. Through case studies of successful financial banking systems using whole life insurance, agents can illustrate the tangible benefits of this approach, inspiring clients to take proactive steps toward crafting a lasting family legacy.

Chapter 12: Case Studies of Successful Financial Banking Systems

Real-Life Examples of Infinite Banking

Real-life examples of infinite banking highlight the practical applications of dividend whole life insurance as a financial tool that supports families in achieving their financial goals. One notable case is the Smith family, who integrated a whole life insurance policy from a mutual company into their financial planning. By utilizing the cash value growth of their policy, they were able to finance their children's education without the need for traditional student loans. The dividends generated from their whole life policy provided a steady income stream, allowing them to borrow against the cash value at favorable rates, thus avoiding high-interest debts and ensuring their financial stability.

Another compelling example is the Johnsons, who used their whole life insurance policy to create an emergency fund. After recognizing the unpredictability of life, they opted to build cash value within their policy that could be accessed in times of need. When an unexpected medical expense arose, they were able to withdraw funds from their policy without the stress of traditional bank loans. This strategy not only provided immediate liquidity but also allowed the Johnsons to continue growing their cash value, demonstrating the effectiveness of whole life insurance as a financial buffer for unforeseen circumstances.

The Garcia family effectively incorporated whole life insurance into their estate planning strategy. By designating their policy as a tool for wealth transfer, they ensured that their heirs would receive a tax-free death benefit. This approach not only facilitated the smooth transition of assets but also allowed the Garcias to leverage their policy's cash value for investment opportunities during their lifetime. Their experience underscores the dual role that whole life insurance can play in both immediate financial planning and long-term legacy building.

In a different scenario, the Parkers utilized the loan features of their dividend whole life insurance to fund a self-sustaining retirement plan. They strategically borrowed against their policy to invest in real estate, generating passive income that supplemented their retirement funds. This case illustrates how individuals can use their whole life policies as a financial banking system, allowing them to create a diversified income stream while still benefiting from the growth of their cash value and dividends.

Lastly, the Williams family serves as a testament to the risk management capabilities of whole life insurance. Faced with potential financial instability due to market volatility, they turned to their whole life policy as a stable asset. By maintaining their policy, they not only secured a death benefit for their dependents but also built a reliable source of funds that could be accessed in times of economic uncertainty. This example emphasizes the importance of whole life insurance as a cornerstone of financial planning that can protect families and provide peace of mind in an ever-changing financial landscape.

Lessons Learned from Successful Policyholders

Successful policyholders of dividend whole life insurance have demonstrated that strategic planning and informed decision-making can significantly enhance financial outcomes. One key lesson learned is the importance of understanding the unique features of whole life policies, particularly those offered by mutual companies. These policies not only provide a death benefit but also accumulate cash value over time, which can be leveraged for various financial needs. Policyholders who took the time to comprehend the mechanics of their policies, including premium payments, dividend payouts, and cash value growth, have often seen substantial financial benefits. They have successfully integrated these policies into their overall financial strategies, ensuring they serve as a cornerstone for building a sustainable financial legacy.

Another critical insight from successful policyholders is the value of maximizing dividend payouts. Those who actively engaged with their insurance agents to understand how dividends are calculated and distributed were able to make more informed choices regarding policy structure and funding. By exploring options such as paid-up additions and flexible premium payments, these policyholders increased their dividend earnings over time. This proactive approach not only enhanced their cash value but also strengthened their financial banking systems, providing them with additional resources to fund emergencies or invest in opportunities without compromising their long-term goals.

The comparison of mutual companies has been essential for many policyholders in selecting the best dividend whole life policies. Successful individuals often shared their experiences, noting that thorough research and comparison of companies regarding their financial strength, historical dividend performance, and customer service reputation played a pivotal role in their choices. By aligning themselves with mutual companies known for consistent and competitive dividend payouts, policyholders were able to enhance the overall effectiveness of their whole life insurance policies. This careful selection process has proven to be a game-changer in establishing reliable financial foundations for their families.

Incorporating whole life insurance into estate planning and wealth transfer strategies has also emerged as a vital lesson. Policyholders who recognized the role of these policies in facilitating smooth transitions of wealth to future generations have taken steps to integrate them into their estate plans. They learned that whole life insurance not only provides liquidity to cover estate taxes and other expenses but also ensures that their heirs receive a tax-free benefit. This foresight has allowed families to preserve their legacies, supporting their loved ones financially without the burden of unexpected costs.

Finally, leveraging the cash value of whole life policies for emergency funds has been a significant takeaway for successful policyholders. Those who understood the loan features of their policies and how to access cash value without triggering adverse tax consequences found themselves better equipped to handle unforeseen financial challenges. This strategic use of cash value not only provides peace of mind but also reinforces the self-funding retirement plans that many policyholders aspire to create. By relying on their whole life insurance policies as a financial safety net, they have been able to maintain stability in their family finances, demonstrating the multifaceted benefits of dividend whole life insurance in long-term financial planning.

Key Takeaways for Implementing Your Own System

Implementing your own financial banking system using dividend whole life insurance requires a strategic approach. The first key takeaway is to thoroughly understand the features of whole life insurance from mutual companies. These policies not only provide death benefits but also build cash value over time through dividends. It's essential to choose a mutual company with a strong track record of consistent dividend payouts, as this will impact both the growth of your cash value and the overall effectiveness of your financial plan. Researching the historical performance and financial stability of various mutual companies can guide you in selecting the best policy to meet your needs.

Maximizing dividend payouts is another crucial aspect of implementing a successful system. Agents and customers should focus on strategies that enhance the growth potential of cash value, such as making additional premium payments or utilizing paid-up additions. These strategies increase both the cash value and the death benefit, allowing for a more robust financial resource. Additionally, understanding how to manage the policy effectively, including timing premium payments and utilizing dividends, can significantly affect the overall performance of the whole life policy.

Incorporating whole life insurance into estate planning and wealth transfer strategies is vital for creating a lasting family legacy. Whole life insurance can play a critical role in providing liquidity for estate taxes and facilitating the transfer of wealth to beneficiaries without the burdens of probate. Agents should educate clients on how to structure policies in conjunction with other estate planning tools, ensuring that the financial banking system not only serves immediate needs but also supports long-term wealth preservation and transfer goals.

The ability to leverage cash value for emergencies or opportunities represents a powerful feature of whole life policies. Establishing a clear understanding of the loan features associated with these policies is essential. When cash value is accessed through policy loans, it can provide a safety net during financial emergencies without disrupting the compounding growth of the policy. However, clients should be aware of the implications of borrowing against the policy and how it can affect both the cash value and death benefit if not managed properly.

Finally, recognizing the tax benefits associated with dividend whole life insurance can greatly enhance a family's long-term savings strategy. The tax-deferred growth of cash value and the tax-free nature of death benefits are significant advantages that should not be overlooked. Life insurance agents must highlight these benefits to clients, reinforcing the idea that whole life insurance is not just a safety net but an integral component of a comprehensive financial legacy plan. By weaving together all these elements, agents and customers can create a robust system that supports financial stability and promotes generational wealth.

Chapter 13: Conclusion

Recap of Key Concepts

In this subchapter, we will recap the essential concepts that underpin the strategic use of dividend whole life insurance as a cornerstone in crafting a family legacy. Life insurance agents and infinite banking customers alike can benefit from understanding how dividend whole life insurance from mutual companies serves not only as a financial safety net but also as a dynamic tool for wealth creation and preservation. By leveraging the features of these policies, individuals can transform their financial landscape, ensuring stability and growth for generations to come.

One of the primary advantages of dividend whole life insurance is its ability to generate dividends, which can significantly enhance cash value over time. Agents should be well-versed in strategies for maximizing these payouts, as they can be reinvested to purchase additional paid-up insurance, effectively increasing both death benefits and cash value. This compounding effect creates a robust financial system that supports the policyholder and their family, providing a reliable source of funds for emergencies, investments, or major life events.

Comparing mutual companies is another critical component of building a successful financial banking system. Different companies offer varied dividend whole life policies, and understanding the nuances of these offerings is essential for agents and customers alike. Factors such as historical performance, financial strength, and customer service should guide the selection process. By choosing a mutual company with a proven track record of strong dividend performance, policyholders can enhance their financial strategies and ensure their legacy is built on solid ground.

Estate planning and wealth transfer are integral aspects of utilizing whole life insurance effectively. These policies can play a pivotal role in providing liquidity to cover estate taxes and ensuring that family assets are passed on without unnecessary financial burden. Additionally, the cash value accumulated can be leveraged for emergency funds or used strategically within a self-funding retirement plan, allowing individuals to maintain their lifestyle while securing their family's future.

Lastly, understanding the loan features of dividend whole life insurance is crucial for comprehensive financial planning. Policyholders can access liquidity through loans against their cash value while still allowing the policy to grow. This dual benefit provides a stable risk management strategy, helping to stabilize family finances during uncertain times. By integrating all these elements, agents and customers can create a robust family financial legacy that not only addresses immediate needs but also supports long-term aspirations.

Next Steps for Readers

As you delve into the realm of whole life insurance and its potential to craft a lasting family legacy, it is essential to take concrete steps to integrate these strategies into your financial plan. Begin by assessing your current financial situation and identifying your family's specific needs. This assessment will serve as the foundation for determining how dividend whole life insurance can enhance your overall financial strategy. Consider consulting with a knowledgeable life insurance agent who specializes in mutual companies to explore suitable policy options that align with your long-term goals.

Understanding the nuances of dividend payouts is crucial for maximizing the benefits of whole life insurance. Research the various mutual companies and their dividend histories to identify which providers consistently offer the best returns. This comparison will empower you to make informed decisions and select a policy that not only meets your immediate needs but also supports your financial objectives over time. Engaging with financial advisors who understand the intricacies of these products can also provide valuable insights into optimizing your dividend payouts.

Incorporating whole life insurance into your estate planning and wealth transfer strategies is another critical step. Evaluate how these policies can facilitate a smoother transition of assets to your heirs while potentially reducing estate taxes. By integrating whole life insurance into your estate plan, you can create a financial legacy that reflects your values and supports your family's future. Take the time to discuss these options with your estate planning attorney to ensure your wishes are clearly articulated and legally binding.

Leveraging the cash value of your whole life policy can serve as an emergency fund, providing financial stability in times of need. Familiarize yourself with the loan features of these policies, as this knowledge will help you navigate how to access funds without jeopardizing your long-term financial health. Additionally, understanding the tax benefits associated with whole life insurance can enhance your long-term savings strategy, allowing you to build a self-funding retirement plan that creates security for you and your family.

Finally, consider examining case studies of successful financial banking systems that have incorporated whole life insurance. These real-life examples can illustrate the transformative potential of these products when used strategically. By learning from others' successes and challenges, you can refine your approach to crafting a family legacy that not only protects your financial future but also empowers your loved ones for generations to come. Take action now to ensure that your family's financial legacy is both strong and enduring.

Encouragement for Building a Legacy

Building a legacy is a profound aspiration that requires thoughtful planning and strategic financial decisions. For life insurance agents and infinite banking customers, the concept of legacy intertwines with the utility of dividend whole life insurance from mutual companies. These policies not only offer death benefits but also serve as a foundation for a robust financial banking system that can support families for generations. By understanding the mechanics of these policies, agents can better educate clients on how to create a lasting impact through their financial choices.

Incorporating whole life insurance into a family financial legacy plan allows families to build wealth that can be passed down. The cash value accumulation within these policies provides a unique opportunity for families to leverage their savings. This can be particularly beneficial in estate planning and wealth transfer strategies. By utilizing the cash value for emergencies or as a funding source for significant life events, families can preserve their wealth while ensuring that future generations have the resources they need to thrive.

Maximizing dividend payouts is crucial for enhancing the financial power of whole life insurance policies. Life insurance agents can play a vital role in guiding clients through the process of selecting mutual companies that offer competitive dividend rates. A well-informed choice can significantly impact the growth of a policy's cash value, thus contributing to the overall financial legacy. Furthermore, understanding the nuances of each mutual company's offerings can empower clients to make decisions that align with their long-term financial goals.

The tax benefits associated with dividend whole life insurance present another compelling reason to incorporate these policies into a financial legacy plan. As families look to build wealth, the potential for tax-deferred growth on the cash value and tax-free death benefits becomes increasingly attractive. This not only enhances the overall value of the policy but also provides a strategic advantage in estate planning, ensuring that more of the family's wealth is preserved for future generations.

Ultimately, the integration of whole life insurance into a legacy plan is about more than just financial products; it reflects a commitment to family and future generations. Life insurance agents have the opportunity to inspire clients to think beyond their immediate financial needs and consider how their choices today will impact their families tomorrow. By building a self-funding retirement plan or stabilizing family finances through risk management, agents can help clients create a legacy that embodies their values and secures their family's financial future.

Recommendations:

To learn more: https://stockmags.com/whole-life-insurance-banking/

Contact Dave at: https://familywealthllc.com/ and tell him Ryan Glenn referred you for your discount.

www.ingramcontent.com/pod-product-compliance
Lightning Source LLC
Chambersburg PA
CBHW070425240526
45472CB00020B/1368